The Little Mermaid

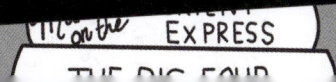

Murder on the ORIENT EXPRESS

THE BIG FOUR

MURDER AT THE VICARAGE

LITTLE WOMEN

FRANKENSTEIN

LENORE
The Raven
POE-MS

THE GREAT GATSBY

AND STILL I RISE

ColouRing Book 1
#2
4

Peter Pa
e Little Whi

POO

EXPRESS

A Literary Bestiary

Edgar Allan Crow & Co

SPECIAL THANKS to Paul, George, Penny, Mum, Dad, Bridget and Jeremy who encouraged, helped and fed me ice cream during the writing of this book.

A Literary Bestiary
Published In 2016 by Jubly-Umph Press

Jubly-Umph Press
PO Box 679
Daylesford Vic
www.jubly-umph.com

Printed in China

ISBN 978-0-646-96256-6

National Library of Australia Cataloguing-in-Publication entry
Creator: Miller, Tasha J., author, illustrator.
Title: A literary bestiary : Edgar Allan Crow & Co / Tasha J Miller, author and illustrator.
ISBN: 9780646962566 (hardback)

Subjects: Anthropomorphism in literature.
Animals in literature.
Poets--Biography--Juvenile literature.
Poets--Juvenile literature--Pictorial works.
Authors--Biography--Juvenile literature.
Authors--Juvenile literature--Pictorial works.

Dewey Number: 808.89282

A Literary Bestiary

Edgar Allan Crow & Co

Words and Illustrations

By Tasha J. Miller

Foreword

One dark winter's day I was brooding, sipping whiskey and pulling out books left and right from my bookshelves, when it occurred to me that I would like to honour my favourite authors in some small way. Piles of novels both new and old surrounded me on the floor and as I picked up an old tome to sniff it (because old books have a marvellously musky odour) I found myself staring into the bleakish face of my literary idol Louisa May Alcott.

I realised, on consideration, that lovely Louisa looked quite like a big brown owl and I thought to myself that I should draw her in anthropomorphic owl form.

So began my project of capturing all my favourite authors and poets and reinventing them as animals with pun-tastic names. Please turn the page and meet Miss Louisa May Owlcott, Edgar Allan Crow, Agatha Twistie and lots of other friends.

The biographies and tales in this book are about real life animal authors and may or may not be historically accurate.

Tasha J Miller

William Shakesteer

B. Apr 26th 1564 (bapt) D. Apr 23rd 1616

William Shakesteer was a master of atmosphere. William Shakesteer was born and raised in a paddock in Stratford-Upon-Avon around 1564. The exact date of his birth and details of his calf-hood are unknown.

In the late 1500s he moved to London to pursue a career as an actor and co-founded the Lord Chamberlain's Steers playing company. His first recorded works are *Richard III* and *Henry VI*. His notable works include the comedies *Much Ado About Nothing, Twelfth Night* and *As You Like It* and tragedies *Romeo and Juliette, Hamlet* and *Macbeth*.

He is considered by many to be the greatest writer in the English language and is often referred to as the "Bard of Avon" or just "The Bard". His poems and plays have been torturing students ever since his death.

"All the world's a stage, and all the men and women merely players."
As You Like It

Jane Austhen

B. Dec 16th 1775 D. Jul 18th 1817

Jane Austhen was a master of the pen. Born into landed gentry in England in 1775, Jane was known for her novels which focus on Georgian sensibilities. Part of a large nest, she remained close to the other chicks all her life. Her novels centre on the dependence of chickens marrying as a means of improving their social standing and financial situation.

Her life mirrored that of many of the characters in her novels. She was reliant on her brothers to support her, and had to move many times as a result of their changing finances.

Her best know novels include *Pride and Prejudice, Emma* and *Sense and Sensibility*. She died in 1817 at the age of 41. Her works have been republished many times as books and plays and have been made into elaborate TV costume dramas.

"Happiness in marriage is entirely a matter of chance."
Pride and Predjudice

Meowy Shelley

B. Aug 30th 1797 D. Feb 1st 1851

Meowy Shelley would scare you silly! Meowy Shelley was an English writer and novelist best known for her gothic horror story *Frankenstein*. She was the second kitten of writer and feminist Meowy Wollstonecraft and political philosopher William Godwin. As a young cat she fell in love with Percy Bysshe Shelley and scandalously ran off with him to Europe.

She wrote her most famous work whilst holidaying on Lake Geneva one dreary summer. Due to poor weather Meowy and friends sat inside reading ghost stories, eating mice and playing games. Inspired by spooky ghost stories they read, a challenge was set to write a modern horror.

The result, which came to her in a dream, was *Frankenstein*. Following the publication of *Frankenstein*, Meowy continued to write until her death of a brain tumour in 1851.

"I beheld the wretch—the miserable monster whom I had created."
Frankenstein

Hams Christian Hamdersen

B. Apr 2nd 1805 D. Aug 4th 1875

Hams Christian wrote some fiction. Hams Christian Hamdersen was a Danish writer best known for his collections of fairytales. Born in a farmyard in Odense in 1805, his early education as a piglet came from the local poor school. He later worked as an apprentice weaver and tailor and at the Royal Danish Theatre before concentrating full time on poetry and writing.

In 1835 Hams published his first collection of fairytales, known in Danish as eventyr, which was not initially successful. It featured tales such as *The Little Mermaid*, T*he Princess and the Pea* and *The Emperor's New Clothes*. The popularity of his fairytales grew over time, and Hams went on to release a second volume of fairytales in 1838. He died in 1875 of liver cancer.

"To be born in a duck's nest, in a farmyard, is of no consequence to a bird, if it is hatched from a swan's egg."
The Ugly Duckling

Edgar Allan Crow

B. Jan 19th 1809 D. Oct 7th 1849

The tale of Crow is a tale of woe. Edgar Allan Crow was hatched in Boston, Massachusetts in 1809. His father abandoned the nest when Edgar was one year old and his mother died shortly thereafter. Raised from then on in the Allan nest, Edgar set to writing stories and poetry.

His first collection, *Tamerlane and Other Poems* was published in 1827 and was largely ignored. Acclaim did not come until much later in life, but he didn't live all that long to enjoy it. He is famous for mysterious and macabre stories, combined with elements of horror, science fiction and spiritualism. He died in New York in 1849 possibly from alcohol abuse or possibly not...

Notable works: *The Tell-Tale Heart*, *The Raven*, *The Fall of The House of Usher* and *Ligeia*

"Deep into that darkness peering, long I stood there, wondering, fearing, Doubting, dreaming dreams no mortal ever dared to dream before."
The Raven

Louisa May Owlcott

B. Nov 29th 1832 D. Mar 6th 1888

Louisa May Owlcott could lay out a plot. Louisa was an American writer, abolitionist and feminist best known for her March Family Saga. Raised by transcendentalist parents in their nest in Concord, Massachusetts, she had a strong bond with her three owlet sisters.

Louisa worked from a young age to help support her family nest. When the American Civil War broke out she flew away to nurse soldiers in Georgetown and the letters from this experience were published as *Hospital Sketches* in 1863.

Louisa's most famous story *Little Women* was loosely based on herself and her sisters. It became an American classic almost immediately. Louisa died in 1888 from a stroke, aged 55.

"She is too fond of books, and it has turned her brain."
Work: A Story of Experience

LITTLE WOMEN

Jay M Barrie

B. May 9th 1860 D. Jun 19th 1937

Jay M Barrie created a fairy. Jay M Barrie was a Scottish playwright and novelist best known for his work *Peter Pan*.

Hatched in Kirriemuir, Scotland in 1860 to a nest of weavers, Jay was one of ten chicks. He was educated at various schools before moving to London as a fledgling to pursue a career in writing. He wrote numerous novels and plays but his most enduring story was of *Peter Pan*, the bird who never grew up.

Peter Pan was originally a play, and then was adapted into a novel. Never a big bird, Jay stood at 5ft 3 1/2 inches. He died in 1937 of pneumonia, and on his death bequeathed the rights to *Peter Pan* to the Great Ormond Street Hospital. They continue to benefit from his bequest to this day.

"Dreams do come true, if only we wish hard enough. You can have anything in life if you will sacrifice everything else for it."
Peter Pan

Agatha Twisty

B. Sep 15th 1890 D. Jan 12th 1976

Agatha Twisty was full of mystery. Often referred to as the 'The Queen of Crime' Agatha's novels were brimming with murder and intrigue. Hatched in Torquay in 1890 Agatha was raised amongst strong and independent snakes and described her own time as a snakelet as being 'very happy'.

During her youth she travelled extensively through Europe and Egypt and set many of her novels in the places she travelled.

Her famous works include the Hercule Poirot books such as *Murder on the Orient Express* and *Death on the Nile* as well as her Miss Marple books such as *The Murder at the Vicarage* and *A Caribbean Mystery*.

She has left behind a library of novels and a very large death tally.

"Imagination is a good servant, and a bad master. The simplest explanation is always the most likely."
The Mysterious Affair At Styles

DEATH ON THE NILE

by Agatha Twistie

F.Spot Fitzgerald

B. Sep 24 1896 D. Dec 21 1940

F. Spot Fitzgerald was a literary herald. F. Spot was an American screenwriter and novelist famous for his works which epitomised the Jazz era. Born in 1896, F. Spot was named after his famous second cousin, Francis Spot Key. He spent his early years as a cub in Buffalo NY before attending Princeton University.

His first novel, *This Side of Paradise*, was published in 1920 and its instant success allowed him and his new wife Zelda to move to Europe, living a decadent lifestyle with other expat Cheetahs.

Lifelong alcoholism finally caught up with him in 1940, and he died from a heart attack in LA aged 44.

"That is part of the beauty of all literature. You discover that your longings are universal longings, that you're not lonely and isolated from anyone. You belong."
Letters from FSF to Sheilah Graham

P.L.Atypus Travers

B. Aug 9th 1899 D. Apr 23th 1996

    P.L.Atypus Travers taught children manners. P.L.Atypus was an Australian hatched British novelist famous for her *Mary Poppins* books about a magical English nanny who goes on adventures with her charges.

    P.L.Atypus spent her early platypup years in northern Qld, Australia where her father worked as a bank clerk. After his death the family moved to NSW where she was educated and began writing and publishing poems.

    She left Australia to pursue an acting career and worked for the British Ministry Of Information during WWII. Her first *Mary Poppins* book was published in 1934 and she went on to publish 7 more in the series. P.L.Atypus died in London in 1996 at the age of 96.

"Michael knew now what was happening to him. He knew he was going to be naughty."
Mary Poppins

George Narwell

B. Jun 25th 1903 D. Jan 21th 1950

George Narwell could write pretty swell. George Narwell was born in the seas of India in 1903 to expat British parents. When he was a calf, his mother returned with him to England along with the other members of their pod. He received a good education at schools such as Eton, and spent many years as a young adult travelling, living with the poor, and writing articles and novels.

His first book *Down and Out in Paris and London* was published in 1933 and is a memoir about his experience of poverty in the two cities.

His most famous works are *Animal Farm*, an anti-Stalinist satire set in a farmyard and *Nineteen Eighty Four*, a dystopian novel about a totalitarian state. George didn't have long to enjoy the fame of his last novel as he died from tuberculosis shortly after publication.

"All animals are equal, but some animals are more equal than others."
Animal Farm

Rooth Park

B. Aug 24th 1917 D. Dec 14th 2010

Rooth Park would leave her mark. Born in Auckland, NZ in 1917 Rooth spent her early years as a joey in the NZ bush exploring, writing and reading. After school she found work as a journalist and then hopped the ditch to continue her career in Sydney.

Her first novel, *A Harp in the South*, concentrated on the poverty experienced by a family of Irish immigrants living in the slums of Sydney. Up to this point, many people denied that slums existed and her work was fundamental in improving housing conditions in the inner city.

She went on to publish many other books such as *Playing Beatie Bow*, *The Muddle Headed Wombat* and two autobiographies.

"He who climbs a cliff may die on the cliff, so what? Always a risk-taker by nature, now I became one by intent."
A Fence Around the Cuckoo

POOR MANS ORANGE

Maya Angelewe

B. Apr 4th 1928 D. May 28th 2014

Maya Angelewe held an interesting view. Born in St Louis, Missouri in 1928 Maya had a disruptive lamb-hood, regularly moving from paddock to paddock. As a young ewe she found work as a fry cook, sex worker, night club dancer and journalist.

Her first autobiography *I Know Why the Caged Bird Sings* was published in 1969 and won her international recognition. She went on to write 6 more autobiographies as well as dozens of books of poetry, plays and articles on civil rights issues.

She has left behind a legacy of works to encourage future young women to be badass.

"You may shoot me with your words, you may cut me with your eyes, you may kill me with your hatefulness, but still, like air, I'll rise!"
And Still I Rise

AND STILL I RISE

About The Author

Tasha Jay Miller

Tasha Jay Miller couldn't get any sillier. Hatched in Melbourne in 1983 Tasha Jay dreamed of being a writer from a young age.

While still a fledgling she studied journalism at Monash University before flying away to see the world. After many years of travel she returned to her home roost, settling in the small town of Daylesford to concentrate on art and writing full time.

Her first book, *Colouring Book #1* was released in 2012 and was soon followed by books *#2, #3* and *#4*. This is her first book with writing in it.

You can follow Tasha Jay's artwork, projects and writing on her website:

WWW.JUBLY-UMPH.COM

The Author: Tasha Jay Miller

FRANKENSTEIN

Pride & Prejudice
EMMA
SENSE & SENSIBILITY

HAMLET
RICHARD III

LENORE
The Raven
POE-MS

POOR MANS ORANG

Peter Pan
The Little White Bird

THE UGLY DUCKLING
The Little Mermaid

ORANGE

MARY POPPINS

1984
ANIMAL FARI